CRAFTING WITH PARACORD

CRAFTING WITH PARACORD

50 FUN AND CREATIVE PROJECTS USING THE WORLD'S STRONGEST CORD

CHAD POOLE

Ulysses Press

Published in the U.S. by
Ulysses Press
P.O. Box 3440
Berkeley, CA 94703
www.ulyssespress.com

ISBN: 978-1-61243-288-5
Library of Congress Control Number 2013957324

Printed in the United States by Bang Printing

10 9 8 7 6 5 4 3 2 1

Acquisitions Editor: Kelly Reed
Managing Editor: Claire Chun
Editor: Lauren Harrison
Proofreader: Elyce Berrigan-Dunlop
Front cover design: Michelle Thompson
Interior design and layout: what!design @ whatweb.com
Cover photos: © Chad Poole

Distributed by Publishers Group West

IMPORTANT NOTE TO READERS: This book is independently authored and published and no sponsorship or endorsement of this book by, and no affiliation with, any trademarked brands or other products mentioned or pictured within is claimed or suggested. All trademarks that appear in ingredient lists, photographs, and elsewhere in this book belong to their respective owners and are used here for informational purposes only. The author and publishers encourage readers to patronize the quality brands mentioned and pictured in this book.

To my parents,
who believed in me when others didn't.
Without your love and support,
I wouldn't be the person I am today.

I would also like to dedicate this book
to the memory of my beloved sister.

Table of Contents

CHAPTER 1

Introduction to Paracord

What Is Paracord?

Since paracord is so versatile, everyone should have a hank lying around for emergency purposes. In this book, you will learn some neat ways to put the paracord to use.

Paracord is simply nylon cord wrapped in a braided sheath. Though it is fairly easy to find paracord, beware of imitation cord. It may look identical to genuine paracord, and the only way to know if it is the real deal is to see the inner strands. Genuine paracord has three to five internal strands. Generic imitation cord may have inner strands, but it won't be like the genuine cord; some may have only one inner strand that is quite large. The paracord that I use is known as 450 and 550; I use two different types depending on the design that I am tying. The 450 paracord has only three inner strands and is not as stiff as 550, which has seven inner strands. This photo shows 450 paracord on the left and 550 on the right.

What Supplies Are Needed for Paracord Designs?

The supplies required are minimal: paracord, scissors, a ruler, and a lighter are the basic items you will need to get started. Other helpful items you might want to obtain are a few curved side-release buckles, lobster clips, and carabiners. An advanced tool that I use is a woodburner pen, which is used to cut and melt the cord at the same time; your final result will look better when using this instead of a lighter.

How Do I Determine How Much Cord Will Be Needed to Tie a Design?

No matter what design you choose to tie, a simple method can be used to determine the length of cord required. Measure the length of a scrap strand of paracord. Then tie a 1-inch-long version of the design you intend to tie. After tying that inch, measure how much cord you have left. Subtract the amount of cord you have left from the length of the total cord. Now take the amount that it takes to tie 1 inch of the design and multiply that by however many inches you intend the design to be.

Introductory Knots

Once you begin tying paracord designs, you will need to determine how to begin or end the design; these knots can be used on almost any bracelet or keychain.

Bracelet Loop

This is how you start a paracord bracelet without using a buckle. The two strands used to tie the loop can be the same or different colors.

1 | Start with the two strands placed vertically beside each other.

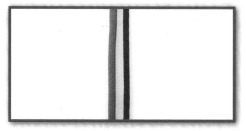

2 | Form a loop with the right red strand and then bring it over the two vertical core strands and under the left blue strand.

3 | Form a loop with the blue strand, bring it over and around the red strand, and then bring it underneath both core strands and out the red loop.

4 | Take the blue strand up, to make a loop, then bring it down through the blue loop on the left side, then under both core strands, under itself, and out the red loop.

5 | Pull the strands tight and adjust the size of the upper loop as needed. The opening needs to be just a bit larger than the intended size of the Bracelet Clasp (page 11) that you intend to tie.

Buckle Starting

You will use this Cow Hitch knot to start most bracelet designs that use a buckle.

1 | Fold the paracord in half and insert it into one end of the buckle.

2 | Insert the free ends of the paracord into the loop and then pull it tight.

Bracelet Clasp

When tying a bracelet without a buckle, you will need a knot on the opposite end of the loop to secure the bracelet to your wrist. This is an intricate way of creating the Bracelet Clasp, but simpler methods are available, such as the Overhand Knot (page 13).

1 | Start with the two strands placed vertically beside each other.

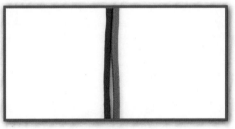

2 | Bring the right blue strand underneath the left red strand and then back around and over the red strand and itself to form a loop.

3 | Bring the red strand around and over the blue strand and then underneath itself and the blue strand and then out the loop of the blue strand.

4 | Form a loop on the right with the blue strand, then bring it over the red strand and itself, then under the red strand and out the loop.

5 | Form a loop on the left with the red strand, then bring it under the blue strand, over itself, then over the blue strand.

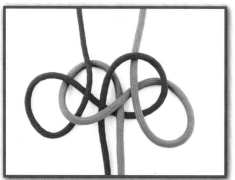

6 | Pull the strands tight.

7 | Cut the remainder of excess cord and melt the ends with a lighter.

Two-Strand Blood Knot

This is another method of starting a bracelet without using a buckle. This method can be used to tie a bracelet loop for a two- or three-strand bracelet.

1 | To tie a three-strand bracelet loop, begin by folding one of the strands in half with the other strand beneath it.

To tie a two-strand bracelet loop, begin by forming a loop with one of the strands (the upper part of the loop will be the long strand, the lower will be short) and the other strand beneath it.

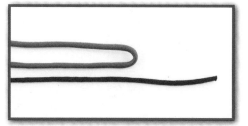

2 | Bring the lower red strand over the other two strands and then around and underneath the other two strands.

3 | Bring the red strand back over all three strands and then around and underneath the three strands, making a loop around the blue strand.

4 | Repeat Step 3.

5 | Insert the red strand up through the middle of the loops created in steps 3 and 4.

6 | Pull on both ends of the red strand. Cut the remainder of the excess red strand (and the short end of the blue strand, if tying a two-strand bracelet) and then melt the end with a lighter.

Overhand Knot

This knot can be used as a simple method of creating a bracelet clasp. It can be tied with multiple strands or a single strand. The two-strand version is shown here.

1 | Form a loop and bring the end over itself.

2 | Then bring it around and underneath itself and out through the loop

3 | Pull both ends to tighten.

CHAPTER 2
Solomon Bars

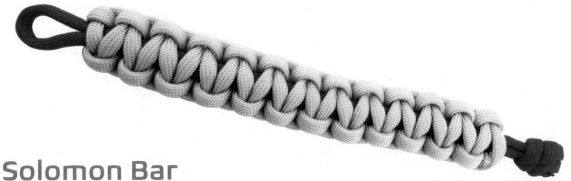

Solomon Bar

If you've seen a paracord bracelet on the Internet or for sale at a store, more than likely the design was a Solomon Bar. While it's known by many names like Cobra Braid, Macramé Bar, or Portuguese Sinnet, it's tied the same way by using a series of left and right half knots.

1 | Start by cutting two strands of paracord, one short strand (about 2 feet long) that will form the red core of the bar, and one long strand (about 6 feet long) for the gray outer knotted section. The finished bracelet will be about 7 inches long.

2 | Find the middle of both strands. Keep the red core strand on the right.

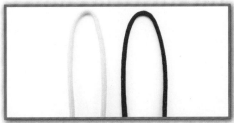

3 | Bring the left strand of the longer gray cord over both red strands and underneath the right gray strand.

4 | Bring the right gray strand underneath both red strands and over the left gray strand.

5 | Pull on the left and right gray strands to tighten; this forms the first half knot.

6 | Bring the right gray strand over the red strands and underneath the left gray strand.

7 | Bring the left gray strand underneath the red strands and over the right gray strand.

8 | Pull on the left and right strands to tighten; this forms the second half knot.

9 | Bring the left gray strand over the red strands and underneath the right gray strand. Bring the right gray strand underneath the red strands and over the gray strand.

10 | Pull on the left and right gray strands to tighten; this forms the third half knot. Keep tying using the same technique to form the half knots until you reach the desired length.

11 | Tie an Overhand Knot (page 13) using the remainder of the core strands.

12 | Finish the design by cutting the remainder of excess cord and melting the end with a lighter.

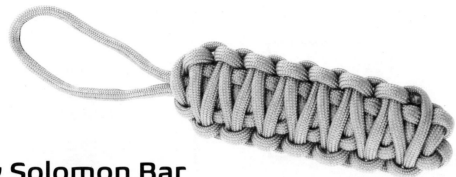

King Solomon Bar

In simple terms, the King Solomon Bar is basically just a doubled Solomon Bar (page 15).

1 | Start by finding the middle of the cord, then form two loops at the intended length of the bar. These will be the core strands.

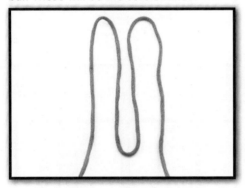

2 | Bring the right cord over the core strands and underneath the left strand.

3 | Bring the left cord underneath the core strands and over the right strand.

4 | Pull on both the left and right strands to tighten the first half knot.

5 | Bring the left cord over the core strands and underneath the right strand. Bring the right cord underneath the core strands and over the left strand.

6 | Pull on both the left and right strands to tighten the second half knot.

7 | Bring the left cord underneath the core strands and over the right strand.

8 | Pull on both the left and right strands to tighten the third half knot.

9 | Continue tying until you reach the desired length. Now you'll go back over the knots you just tied, tying half knots over the whole Solomon Bar rather than simply the core strands. Bring the left cord over the Solomon Bar you just tied and underneath the right strand. Bring the right cord underneath the Solomon Bar and over the left strand. Important: Make sure your starting point looks like the photo.

10 | Pull on both the left and right strands to tighten the half knot.

11 | Bring the right cord over the Solomon Bar and underneath the left strand. Bring the left cord underneath the Solomon Bar and over the right strand.

12 | Pull on both the left and right strands to tighten the half knot.

13 | Keep tying until you reach the bottom of the Solomon Bar.

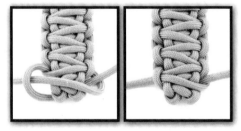

14 | Cut the remainder of the excess cord and melt the ends with a lighter.

Solomon Bar Watchband

This is a basic Solomon Bar (page 15) tied as a watchband.

1 | Start by cutting four strands, two short strands about 14 inches long, and two long strands about 7 feet long. You may want to bend the watch pins outward in order for the paracord to fit.

2 | Lay the watch out to see how it will be tied.

3 | Run one of the short strands between the buckle and the watch pin and then tie a half knot (as shown in the Solomon Bar, page 15) to secure it in place. Make sure the length will be exactly half the length required for the full length of the watchband.

4 | Now do the opposite on the other end of the watch.

5 | Start on one side of the watch by tying a half knot over the core strands by bringing the left strand underneath the core strands and the right strand over the core strands and under the left strand.

6 | Pull on the left and right strands to tighten the knot.

7 | Tie another half knot and then tighten.

8 | Continue tying half knots until you reach the buckle.

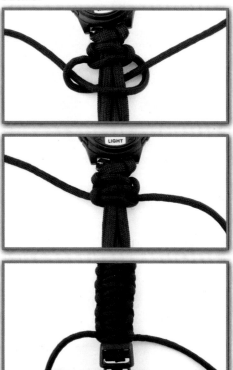

9 | Now tie half knots over the core strands of the opposite side of the watchband and continue until you have reached the buckle.

10 | Cut the remainder of the excess cord and melt the ends with a lighter.

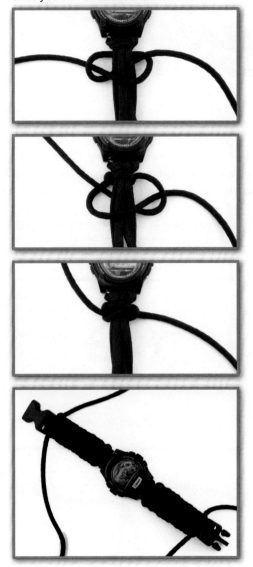

Stitched Solomon Bar

Unlike many of the other Solomon Bar designs, this is relatively new and was originally tied by J. D. Lenzen. Lenzen pioneered the method of knot tying called fusion knotting, a method of merging elements to create innovative knots.

1 | Start by cutting strands of paracord, one short strand (about 2 feet long) that will form the blue core of the bar, and one long strand (about 7 feet long) for the gray outer knotted section.

Find the middles of the two cords.

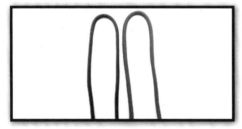

2 | Wrap the gray cord around the blue core strands.

3 | Bring the right gray strand underneath the blue strands and over the left gray strand. Bring the left gray strand over the blue strands and under the right gray strand.

4 | Pull the left and right gray strands to tighten the knot.

5 | Bring the right gray strand underneath the right blue strand and over the left blue strand and then under the left gray strand.

6 | Bring the left gray strand underneath both the blue strands and over the right gray strand.

7 | Pull the left and right gray strands to tighten the knot.

8 | Bring the left gray strand underneath the left blue strand and over the right blue strand and then under the right gray strand.

9 | Bring the right gray strand underneath both blue strands and over the left gray strand.

10 | Pull the left and right gray strands to tighten the knot.

11 | Bring the right gray strand underneath the right blue strand and over the left blue strand and then under the left gray strand.

12 | Bring the left black strand underneath both blue strands and over the right gray strand.

13 | Pull the left and right gray strands to tighten the knot.

14 | Bring the left gray strand underneath the left blue strand and over the right blue strand and then over the right gray strand. Bring the right gray strand underneath both blue strands and over the left gray strand.

15 | Pull the left and right gray strands to tighten the knot.

16 | Continue tying until you reach the desired length and then tie an Overhand Knot (page 13) using the blue core strands.

17 | Cut the remainder of the excess cord and melt the ends with a lighter.

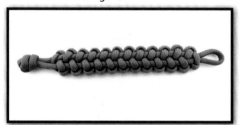

Striped Solomon Bar

The Striped Solomon Bar is another modification of the versatile Solomon Bar. It can be tied with or without a buckle, but the buckle helps make this a better-looking design. Use the first chapter to determine how to measure your wrist to decide how long the bracelet will need to be.

1 | Start with a 2⅓-foot white and a 7-foot gray cord.

2 | Start by tying the gray cord in a Cow Hitch (see Buckle Starting on page 11) around one side of the buckle, then tighten the knot

3 | Measure the distance you need the bracelet to be and then tie a Cross Knot (page 109) around the other side of the buckle.

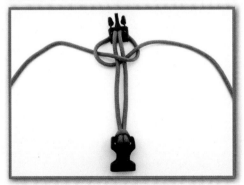

4 | Tie a second Cross Knot. Wrap the white core cord around the square knot, directly between the two core gray strands. The key to tying this design is to keep the same cord on top and the other on the bottom.

5 | Tighten the Cross Knot. Now tie another square knot, this time placing the white cord underneath.

6 | Tighten the Cross Knot.

7 | Tie another Cross Knot with the white cord on top.

8 | Tighten the knot.

9 | Tie another Cross Knot with the white cord underneath.

10 | Continue tying Cross Knots, moving the white cord under and over the gray knots. Once you reach the other buckle, cut the center cord as shown.

11 | Tie a Cross Knot to cover the center cord.

12 | Tighten the knot.

13 | Depending on your bracelet, you may want to add another Cross Knot above the buckle.

14 | Cut the remainder of the excess cord and melt the ends with a lighter.

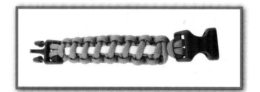

Twisted Solomon Bar

This is tied almost exactly like the basic Solomon Bar (page 15), the difference being that you reverse each half knot instead of keeping the same cord atop the core.

1 | Start by finding the middle of the cord, then form two loops at the intended length of the bar.

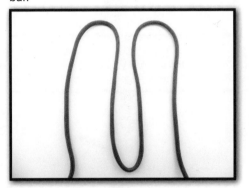

2 | Bring the right strand over both the core strands and underneath the left strand.

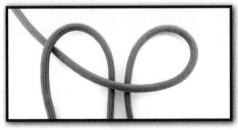

3 | Bring the left strand underneath both core strands and over the right strand.

4 | Pull the left and right strands to tighten the knot.

5 | Bring the left strand underneath both core strands and over the right strand.

6 | Bring the right strand over both core strands and underneath the left strand.

7 | Pull the left and right strands to tighten the knot.

8 | Bring the left strand underneath both core strands and over the right strand.

9 | Bring the right strand over both core strands and underneath the left strand.

10 | Pull the left and right cords to tighten the knot.

11 | Continue the same technique: left strand underneath both core strands and over the right strand. Bring the right strand over both core strands and underneath the left strand.

12 | Pull the left and right cords to tighten the knot.

13 | Continue tying until you have a small loop at the end of the core.

14 | Cut the remainder of the excess cord and melt the ends with a lighter.

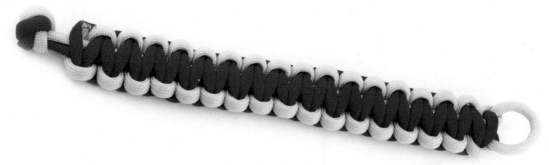

Two-Color Solomon Bar

This design adds a little color to the plain Solomon Bar (page 15), and aside from the beginning steps, it's tied the same way.

1 | Tie a Bracelet Loop (page 10) with two different colored cords.

2 | Pull the knot tight.

3 | Bring the red left strand over the core strands to the opposite side. Then bring the right silver strand over and around the red strand, and then underneath the core strands to the left and out the red loop.

4 | Pull both strands outward to tighten the knot.

5 | Bring the red strand over the core strands to the opposite side. Then bring the silver strand over and around the red strand, and then underneath the core strands to the right and out the loop.

6 | Pull both strands outward to tighten the knot.

7 | Repeat steps 3 through 6, and continue tying until you've reached the desired length. Then use the core strands and tie a Bracelet Clasp (page 11), or as shown in the image, an Overhand Knot (page 13).

CHAPTER 3

Bracelets, Bars, & Keychains

Alligator Fang

This is one of many designs included in this book that was originally created by DMan, a talented paracord-tying artist. His work can be found throughout the Internet. The Alligator Fang will work easily as a bracelet, keychain, or strap.

1 | Begin by tying a Bracelet Loop (page 10) with green and gray cords, then pull the loop tight.

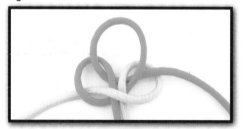

2 | Bring the right green strand under the gray core strand, over the green core strand, and then under the left strand.

3 | Bring the left gray strand under the green core strand, over the gray core strand, and out through the green loop.

4 | Continuing with the gray strand, wrap the cord underneath and out the green loop.

5 | This image shows the full path the gray strand should take.

6 | Pull the green and gray strands tight.

7 | Starting with the green strand, bring it under the green core strand and over the gray core strand, and then under the gray strand.

8 | Bring the gray strand under and over the core strands.

9 | Continuing with the gray strand, bring it around, under, and out the loop of the green strand as shown.

10 | Pull the left and right strands tight. Repeat steps 2 through 7, and continue tying until you've reached the desired length.

11 | Once you've reached the end, secure the ends by tying two half knots as if tying a Solomon Bar (page 15). Tie an Overhand Knot (page 13) using the two core strands to make a button for the bracelet.

12 | Cut the remainder of the excess cord and melt the ends with a lighter to finish the bracelet.

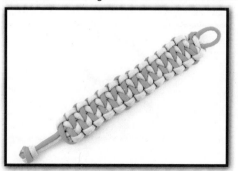

Bracelets, Bars, & Keychains

The Barb Branch Tie

Originally created by DMan, this design is not too thick and can be used as a bracelet or strap.

1 | Start by forming a loop in the middle section of the red cord.

2 | Bring the brown cord over and around loop in the red cord.

3 | Now pass the loose ends of the brown cord through the loop previously formed to create a Cow Hitch (see Buckle Starting on page 11).

4 | Tighten the Cow Hitch.

5 | Cross the red cord underneath the brown cord.

6 | Bring the right strand of the brown cord around and underneath the red cord, then go over itself and then underneath the red cord again.

7 | Tighten the brown cord and then pull both strands of the red cord to tighten.

8 | Cross the first red cord underneath the brown cord.

9 | Bring the left strand of the brown cord around and underneath the red cord, then go over itself and then underneath the red cord again.

10 | Tighten the brown cord and then pull both strands of the red cord to tighten.

11 | Repeat steps 5 through 10, and continue tying until you've reached the desired length.

12 | Bring the right strand of the red cord over the brown cord and under the left red strand. Then bring the left red strand underneath the brown cord and out the loop of the right red cord to form two Half Knots (see tying a Solomon Bar, page 15).

13 | Pull both strands of the red cord to tighten the Half Knots.

14 | Tie an Overhand Knot (page 13) or a Bracelet Clasp (page 11).

15 | Pull the knot tight.

16 | Cut the excess remainder of the cord and melt the ends with a lighter.

Barbwire

Many of the designs in this chapter were created by Matthias Agnello, including this tutorial. Matthias's work has been gaining popularity and for good reason; this talented artist has created many exceptional paracord designs.

1 | Start by tying a Bracelet Loop (page 10) with silver and blue cords.

2 | Pull the strands tight to secure the loop.

3 | Bring the right silver strand under the blue core strand, over the silver core strand, and then over the left blue strand.

4 | Loop the blue strand around the silver strand and then under and over the core strands.

5 | Bring the blue strand around and back through the silver strand loop to form a loop.

6 | Pull both strands tight to secure the first section of the design.

7 | Bring the silver strand under and over the core strands and then over the blue strand.

8 | Bring the blue strand over the silver strand, under the blue core strand, under the silver strand and over the silver core strand.

9 | Bring the blue strand around and back through the silver strand loop to form a loop.

10 | Pull both strands tight to secure the second section of the design.

11 | Repeat steps 3 through 10, and continue tying until you've reached the desired length. Tie two Half Knots as if tying a Solomon Bar (page 15) to secure the design.

12 | Pull both strands tight.

13 | Use the remainder of the core strands to tie a button for the bracelet. Cut the remainder of the excess cord and melt the ends with a lighter.

Braced Shark Jaw Bone

Another design originally created by Matthias Agnello, this tutorial shows how to tie the design as a bracelet or keychain.

1 | Start by tying a Bracelet Loop (page 10) with green and blue cords.

2 | Pull the strands tight. If you are tying a bracelet, keep the pictured loop. Otherwise, remove the loop by pulling the right strand tight.

3 | Bring the green strand over the blue core strand, under the green core strand, and under the blue strand.

4 | Bring the blue strand over both core strands and then form a loop inside the loop of the green strand as shown.

5 | Bring the blue strand around and through the open loop formed in step 5.

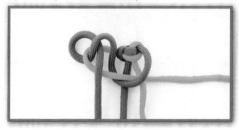

6 | Pull both strands tight to form the first section of the design.

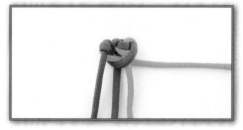

7 | To begin the second section, bring the green strand over and under the core strands and then under the blue strand.

8 | Bring the blue strand over both core strands and then form a loop inside the loop of the green strand as shown.

9 | Bring the blue strand around and through the open loop formed in step 9.

10 | Pull both strands tight to form the second section of the design.

11 | Continue alternating between the first and second sections to complete the length of the design. To lock the design in place, tie two Half Knots, as if tying a Solomon Bar (page 15).

12 | Pull both strands tight. If tying a bracelet, or to add a decorative look to a keychain, tie a couple of Wall Sinnets (page 111) using the remainder of the core strands. Cut the remainder of the excess cord and melt the ends with a lighter.

The Chainlink Bar

Originally created by DMan, this is another design that can be used as a bracelet, strap, or leash.

1 | Start by tying a Bracelet Loop (page 10).

2 | Tighten the Bracelet Loop.

3 | Bring the right gray strand over the red core strand and then underneath and back out.

4 | Now bring the gray strand up and over itself and both the core strands, then bring it underneath the core strands and then back out the loop you just made.

5 | Tighten the right strand, completing the right stitch.

6 | Bring the red strand over the gray core strand and then underneath and back out.

7 | Now bring the red strand up and over itself and the core strands, then bring it underneath the core strands, and then back out the loop you just made.

8 | Tighten the left strand, completing the left stitch.

9 | Repeat steps 3 through 8, and continue tying left and right stitches to complete the design.

10 | Once you've reached the desired length, secure the design in place with two Half Knots, as if tying a Solomon Bar (page 15). Use the remainder of the core strands to tie a Bracelet Clasp (page 11) or a Wall Sinnet (page 111) as shown here.

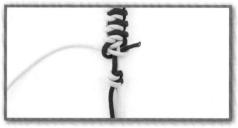

11 | Cut the remainder of the excess cord and melt the ends with a lighter.

The Chainsaw Bar

Originally created by Matthias Agnello, this is a thick design with an aggressive look that will create a terrific bracelet or keychain.

1 | Start by tying a Bracelet Loop (page 10) with red and gray cords.

2 | Tighten the Bracelet Loop, leaving a small loop at the top.

3 | Bring the left gray strand over both core strands and under the red strand.

4 | Bring the red strand over the gray strand and the right gray core strand, then underneath both gray strands, and then back out.

5 | Bring the red strand over itself, under both core strands, and out the loop of the gray strand.

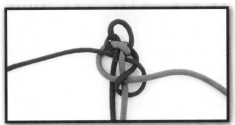

6 | Pull both strands tight to securely tighten the knot.

7 | Bring the gray strand (now on the right) over both core strands and under the red strand.

8 | Bring the red strand over the gray strand and the red core strand, then underneath both strands, and then back out.

9 | Bring the red strand over itself, under both the core strands, and out the loop of the gray strand.

10 | Pull both strands tight to securely tighten the knot.

11 | Repeat steps 3 through 10, and continue tying until you've reached the desired length.

12 | Bring the right red strand over both core strands and underneath the gray strand. Then bring the left strand underneath both core strands and out the loop of the red strand, forming two Half Knots as if tying a Solomon Bar (page 15). Use the remainder of the core strands to tie a Bracelet Clasp (page 11) or an Overhand Knot (page 13) as seen here.

13 | Tighten the Half Knots. Cut the remainder of the excess cord and melt the ends with a lighter.

The Clove & Dagger Bar

Another design by DMan, this thick bar would make an excellent bracelet or strap.

1 | Start with two cords. Make a loop in the middle of the gray cord. Find the middle of the white cord and bring it over and through the gray loop.

2 | Now insert the loose ends of the white cord through the white loop to make a Cow Hitch (see Buckle Starting on page 11) and then pull the cords tight.

3 | Cross the gray cords underneath the white cords.

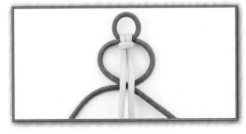

4 | Bring the right white cord underneath the gray cords to the make a loop to the right, bringing the white cord back out the gray loop and over itself.

5 | Bring the white cord over itself to the left, then underneath the gray cords and then back out the gray loop and under the white cord toward the right.

6 | Tighten the white cord.

7 | Bring the left white cord underneath the gray cords to make a loop to the left, bringing the white cord back out the gray loop.

8 | Bring the white cord over itself to the right, then underneath the gray cords and then back out the gray loop and under the white cord toward the left.

9 | Tighten the cords, completing the first row.

10 | Cross the gray cords underneath the white cords.

11 | Bring the right white cord underneath the gray cords to make a loop to the left, bringing the white cord back out the gray loop.

12 | Bring the right cord over itself to the right, then underneath the gray cords and then back out the gray loop and under the right cord toward the left.

13 | Tighten the white cord.

14 | Bring the left white cord underneath the gray cords to make a loop to the right, bringing the white cord back out the gray loop.

15 | Bring the white cord over itself to the left, then underneath the gray cords and then back out the gray loop and under the white cord toward the right.

16 | Tighten the white cord, completing the second row.

17 | Repeat steps 4 through 16, and continue tying until you've reached the desired length.

18 | Finish by tying a Bracelet Clasp (page 11).

19 | Cut the remainder of the excess cord and melt the ends with a lighter.

The Crossing Tongues Bar

Originally created by DMan, this is a thick design and would make an excellent bracelet or keychain.

1 | Start with two cords. Make a loop in the middle of the gray cord. Find the middle of the orange cord and bring it over and through the gray loop.

2 | Now insert the loose ends of the orange cord through the orange loop to make a Cow Hitch (see Buckle Starting on page 11) and then pull the cords tight.

3 | Bring the left gray strand over and under the orange core strands and then over the right gray strand.

4 | Wrap the left gray strand around the right gray strand, and then bring it underneath the right strand and then under and over the core strands and then out and over itself.

5 | Tighten the gray strands, pushing the knot up to help hold it in place.

6 | Bring the right gray strand over and under the orange core strands and then over the left gray strand.

7 | Wrap the right gray strand around the left gray strand and then bring it underneath the left strand and then under and over the core strands and then out and over itself.

8 | Tighten the gray strands, pushing the knot up to help hold it in place.

9 | Repeat steps 5 through 10, and continue tying until you've reached the desired length.

10 | Bring the right gray strand over the orange core strands and under the left gray strand. Bring the left gray strand under the core strands and out the loop of the right strand to form two Half Knots as if tying a Solomon Bar (page 15).

11 | Pull both gray strands tight.

12 | Tie two more Half Knots.

13 | Pull both strands tight.

16 | Add a Wall Sinnet (page 111) to the core strands to add a decorative touch. Cut the remainder of the excess cord and melt the ends with a lighter.

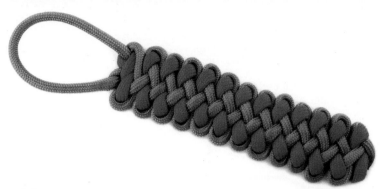

Dragon's Claw

Here's another design originally created by Matthias Agnello.

1 | Start with two pieces of cord and tie them in a Bracelet Loop (page 10).

2 | Pull the strands tight to secure the loop. Bring the left orange cord over and under the core strands. Bring the right brown cord over the core strands.

3 | Bring the brown cord up, around, and back through the orange loop.

4 | Pull both strands tight to secure the first section of the design.

5 | Bring the orange strand over and under the core strands. Then bring the brown strand over the core strands and back through the orange loop.

6 | Pull both strands tight to secure the second section of the design.

7 | Repeat steps 2 through 6, and continue tying until you've reached the desired length. Tie two Half Knots as if tying a Solomon Bar (page 15) to secure the design. Pull both strands tight. Cut the remainder of the excess cord and melt the ends with a lighter.

Genoese Bar

This classic design was described as far back as the 1940s by Clifford Ashley.

1 | Start with two cords and find the middle of each one. Loop the gray cord over the green cord.

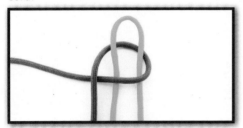

2 | Form two Half Knots with the gray cord as if tying a Solomon Bar (page 15).

3 | Pull both gray strands tight.

4 | Bring the left gray strand over the green core strands and then bring it back underneath the core strands and out the gray loop.

5 | Pull the knot tight to complete the first section of the design.

6 | Bring the right gray strand over the core strands and then bring it back underneath the core strands and out the gray loop.

7 | Pull the knot tight to complete the second section of the design.

8 | Repeat steps 4 through 7, and continue tying until you've reached the desired length.

9 | Tie two Half Knots to secure the design. Using the remainder of the green core strands, tie an Overhand Knot (page 13) to make a button for the bracelet. Cut the remainder of the excess cord and melt the ends with a lighter.

Ladder Rack Knot

This design has been around for a while. This is the way that was originally shown by Bud Brewer.

1 | Start by forming three loops in the cord. Make sure that the left and right strands are equal lengths. The center loop will need to be the full length of the design, which will include the keychain loop.

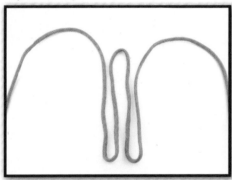

2 | Bring the right strand over both core strands and underneath the left strand. Bring the left strand underneath both core strands and then out and over the right strand. The top loop will be the keychain loop and the bottom section will be the knotted section of the design.

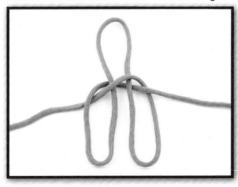

3 | Bring the left strand out and over the left loop and underneath both core strands and then out and over the right loop.

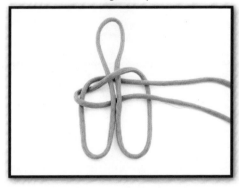

4 | Bring the right strand out and underneath the right loop and then over both core strands and then underneath the left loop.

5 | Repeat steps 3 and 4, and continue tying until you've reached the bottom loops.

6 | Pull the keychain loop and push down on the knot section to tighten the knot. Then carefully work the strands on both sides by starting from the top and working toward the bottom.

7 | Cut the remainder of the excess cord and melt the ends with a lighter.

Padded Pagoda

Another design by Matthias Agnello, this can be tied as a keychain or bracelet.

1 | Begin by tying a Bracelet Loop (page 10) with brown and gray cords. Tighten the knot.

2 | Bring the left brown strand underneath the two core strands and over the right gray strand. Bring the gray strand over the two core strands and then over and back down and out the loop of the brown strand. Pull both strands tight.

3 | Bring the brown strand underneath the two core strands and over the gray strand. Bring the gray strand over the two core strands, and then make a loop by bringing the strand around the backside of the brown right strand and then underneath itself and down.

4 | Pull both strands tight.

5 | Bring the brown strand underneath the two core strands and over the gray strand. Bring the gray strand over the two core strands and then make a loop by bringing the strand around the backside of the brown strand and then underneath itself and down.

6 | Pull both strands tight.

7 | Repeat steps 2 through 6, and continue tying until you've reached the desired length.

8 | Tie two Half Knots as if tying a Solomon Bar (page 15) to secure the design in place.

9 | Pull both strands tight. If you are tying a bracelet, use the remaining two core strands and tie a Bracelet Clasp (page 11) for the loop, then cut the remainder of the excess cord and melt the ends. If you are tying a keychain, cut the excess of the two core strands and melt the ends with a lighter. Finish the design by trimming the remaining cord from the half knots you tied in step 8, then melt the ends with a lighter.

Sawtooth Volume I

Originally created by Matthias Agnello, this thick design can be used as a bracelet, but it would work better as a strap or keychain.

1 | Start by tying a Bracelet Loop (page 10) with red and gray cords.

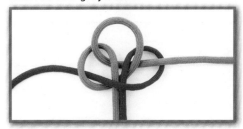

2 | Pull both strands to tighten the Bracelet Loop.

3 | Bring the left red strand over the two core strands and under the right gray strand.

4 | Bring the gray strand over the red strand, then under the red core strand and over the gray core strand and then over and out the red strand.

5 | Bring the gray strand up and around the backside of the red strand and then out the red loop.

6 | Pull both strands tight.

7 | Bring the red strand over the two core strands and then under the gray strand.

8 | Bring the gray strand over the red strand, then under the gray core strand and over the red core strand and then out and over the red strand.

9 | Bring the gray strand up and around the backside of the right strand and then out the red loop.

10 | Pull both strands tight.

11 | Repeat steps 3 through 10, and continue tying until you've reached the desired length.

12 | Tie two Half Knots as if tying a Solomon Bar (page 15) to secure the design in place.

13 | Pull both strands tight.

14 | Tie a Bracelet Clasp (page 11) using the remainder of the excess core strands.

15 | Pull the Bracelet Clasp tight and the cut off the remainder of the core strands. Melt the ends with a lighter.

Single Tatted Bar

This simple design works well as a keychain.

1 | Make a loop in a single piece of cord. This loop will need to be the length of the intended design.

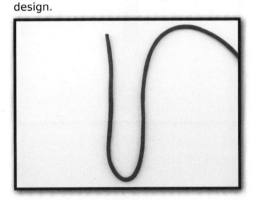

2 | Bring the strand back around on itself and then over the core strand.

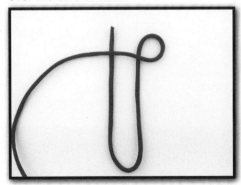

3 | Bring the strand up and underneath the core strands and out the loop made in step 2.

4 | Pull the knot tight.

5 | Bring the strand over the core strands and then up and back under the core strands and out the loop.

6 | Bring the core strand that is sticking out at the top back down and inside the knot.

7 | Pull the knot tight.

8 | Bring the strand under the core strands and then back over the core strands and out the loop.

9 | Pull the knot tight.

10 | Repeat steps 8 and 9, and continue tying until you've reached the desired length.

11 | Cut the remainder of the excess cord and melt the ends with a lighter.

Surreal Sawtooth Bar

Originally created by Matthias Agnello, this is a thick design that can be used as a bracelet or keychain.

1 | Start by tying a Bracelet Loop (page 10) with blue and silver cords.

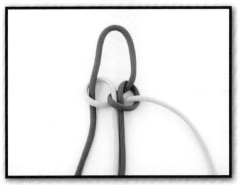

2 | Pull the Bracelet Loop tight. If tying a bracelet, leave a smaller loop; use a larger loop for a keychain (as shown in the image).

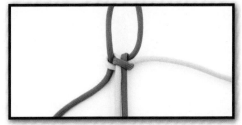

3 | Bring the right silver strand underneath the blue core strand and over the silver core strand. Then bring it around and underneath the silver core strand and over the blue core strand.

4 | Bring the silver strand over, around, and underneath itself and out the loop and down.

5 | Pull the knot tight.

6 | Bring the blue strand under the silver core strand and over the blue core strand. Then bring it around and underneath the blue core strand and over the silver core strand.

7 | Bring the blue strand over, around, and underneath itself and out the loop and down.

8 | Pull the knot tight. Repeat steps 3 through 7 and continue tying until you've reached the desired length.

9 | At the bottom of the bar, tie two Half Knots as if tying a Solomon Bar (page 15), by bringing the left strand over the center strands and the right strand underneath the two center strands and out the loop.

10 | Pull the knot tight. Cut the remainder of the excess cord and melt the ends with a lighter.

The Tap-Out Bar

This unique design was originally created by DMan and can be used as a thick bracelet or keychain.

1 | Start by tying a Bracelet Loop (page 10) with blue and gray cords.

2 | Pull the strands to tighten the Bracelet Loop.

3 | Bring the right gray strand over the right blue core strand and then underneath and out the loop.

4 | Run the gray strand underneath itself and the right core strand then over itself, the left core strand, and the left blue strand.

5 | Bring the blue strand under the left gray core strand and the gray right strand, and then bring it back over and underneath itself to form a loop.

6 | Now bring the blue strand up and over itself, under both core strands, and then bring it through both loops of the gray strand.

7 | Tighten the strands to complete the first row.

8 | Start the second row by bringing the gray strand underneath the left gray core strand and then over and out the loop.

9 | Bring the gray strand up and over itself, under the gray core strand, and over the blue core strand.

10 | Bring the blue strand over the left strand and the blue core strand, then underneath the right core strand and out the loop.

11 | Bring the blue strand underneath itself, the blue core strand, the gray core strand, and the right gray strand, then bring it out the loop of the left strand.

12 | Tighten the strands to complete the second row.

13 | Repeat steps 3 through 12, and continue tying until you've reached the desired length.

14 | Bring the left strand over both core strands, and then bring the right strand underneath the core strands to form two Half Knots as if tying a Solomon Bar (page 15). Tie the remainder of the core strands in a Bracelet Clasp (page 11) or a Wall Sinnet (page 111) as shown here. Finish off the bracelet by cutting the excess cord and melting the ends with a lighter.

Double Tatted Chain

This design makes a thick bracelet or could also be used for a leash. It requires two separate cords.

1 | Start with two cords. Tie a Slip Knot (see Chain Sinnet, page 75) in the white cord.

2 | Tighten the Slip Knot to form the loop for the bracelet.

3 | Tie the black cord in a Cow Hitch (see Buckle Starting on page 11) around the first cord.

4 | Tighten the Cow Hitch.

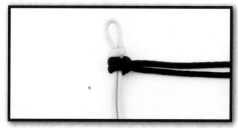

5 | Bring both black strands over both white strands and then underneath the white strands and out the loop.

6 | Tighten the black cord.

7 | Bring both white strands around and over the black strands and then underneath the black strands and out the loop.

8 | Tighten the white cord.

9 | Bring both black strands around and over both white strands and then underneath the white strands and out the loop.

10 | Tighten the black cord.

11 | Bring both white strands around and over the black strands and then underneath the black strands and out the loop.

12 | Tighten the white cord.

13 | Repeat steps 9 through 12, and continue tying until you've reached the desired length. If tying a bracelet, finish up with a simple Overhand Knot (page 13) or a Bracelet Clasp (page 11). Cut the remainder of the excess cord and melt the ends with a lighter.

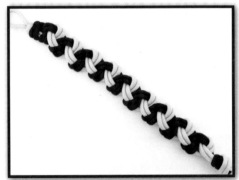

Single Tatted Chain

This is tied exactly the same way as the Double Tatted Chain (page 67) without the additional cord, making it less bulky.

1 | Start by making a loop in the middle of the cord.

2 | Form a loop with the strand on the right and then bring it underneath and through the first loop to make a Slip Knot (see Chain Sinnet, page 75).

3 | Tighten the loop.

4 | Bring the right strand over the left, around and then back underneath the left, and out the loop.

5 | Bring the left strand over the right, around and then back underneath the right, and out the loop.

6 | Tighten both strands.

7 | Bring the right strand over the left, around, and then back underneath the left and out the loop.

8 | Bring the left strand over the right, around, and then back underneath the right and out the loop.

9 | Tighten both strands.

10 | Repeat steps 7 through 9, and continue tying until you've reached the desired length.

11 | Finish it off with a simple Overhand Knot (page 13) or Bracelet Clasp (page 11). Cut the remainder of the excess cord and melt the ends with a lighter.

The Zipper Bar

This design was originally created by DMan and can be used as a bracelet or strap.

1 | Start by tying a Bracelet Loop (page 10) with white and red cords.

2 | Pull the strands to tighten the Bracelet Loop.

3 | Bring the white strand underneath the red core strand and then back over the core and itself.

4 | Bring the white strand under itself and both core strands.

5 | Bring the red strand under the white strand, then over both core strands and through the loop of the white strand.

6 | Tighten the strands to complete the first row.

7 | Bring the white strand under the white core strand and then over the core and itself.

8 | Bring the white strand under itself and both core strands and then over the red strand.

9 | Bring the red strand over both core strands and through the loop of the white strand.

10 | Tighten the strands to complete the second row.

11 | Repeat steps 3 through 10, and continue tying until you've reached the desired length.

12 | Tie a Bracelet Clasp (page 11) using the two core strands. Cut the remainder of the excess cord and melt the ends with a lighter.

CHAPTER 4

Practical Ropecraft

Blood Knot

This is a functional knot, but you can use it to add a loop to the end of a design.

1 | Form a backward "S" shape with the cord.

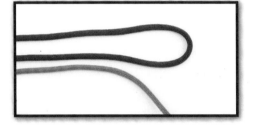

2 | Bring the bottom cord over the upper section and then back around.

3 | Make a couple of loops around the upper section.

4 | Insert the free end of the cord through the center of the loops you just created.

5 | Pull the cord tight to finish off the knot.

6 | Cut the remainder of the excess cord and melt the ends with a lighter.

Chain Sinnet

This is one of the first bracelets I learned to tie. It's an easy design that can be quickly unraveled by loosening the ends and pulling it like a zipper.

1 | Find the middle of the cord and make a loop with the right strand over the left.

2 | Form a loop with the right strand and then insert it into the loop created in step 1. This will create a Slip Knot.

3 | Pull down on the loop you just created to create another loop; this will be the bracelet loop.

4 | Form a loop with the left strand and then insert it into the top loop.

5 | Pull the right strand to tighten the knot.

6 | Form a loop with the right strand and then insert it into the top loop. Pull the left strand to tighten the knot.

7 | Form a loop with the left strand and then insert it into the top loop. Pull the right cord to tighten the knot.

8 | Repeat steps 6 and 7, and continue tying until you've reached the desired length.

9 | To lock the cord, instead of forming a loop, insert the one entire strand into the top loop.

10 | Pull on the opposite cord to tighten the knot.

11 | Use the remaining cord to tie an Overhand Knot (page 13) to secure the bracelet. Cut the remaining cord and melt the ends with a lighter.

Flashlight Wrap

For this project you'll need a 3-inch flashlight and 10 to 12 feet of paracord.

1 | Tie a simple Overhand Knot (page 13) around the flashlight.

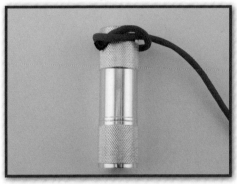

2 | Carefully pull the knot tight, making sure to leave as little cord as possible underneath the knot.

3 | Wrap the cord around the backside of the flashlight and then through the loop.

4 | Pull the knot tight.

5 | Wrap the cord around the backside of the flashlight and then through the loop.

6 | Pull the knot tight.

7 | Repeat steps 5 and 6, continuing to wrap the cord around the flashlight until you've reached the bottom of the flashlight. Cut the remainder of the excess cord and melt the end with a lighter.

Germ Grenade

This useful design is meant to be used for a small bottle of hand sanitizer, but it can be adapted for other types of bottles.

1 | Find the middle of an 8-foot length of cord and wrap it around the neck of the bottle.

2 | Bring the cord around to the other side and insert the cord inside the loop. A rubber band wrapped around the bottle can make it easier to hold the cord on the bottle.

3 | Flip the bottle around to the opposite side. Bring the strand on the left side around and form a loop, then insert the loop underneath the core strands.

4 | Bring the strand on the right side through the loop of the left strand, over the core strands, and then underneath the left strand.

5 | Continuing with that same strand, bring it over the core strands and through the loop of the left strand.

6 | Pull the left and right strands outward to tighten the knot.

7 | Flip the bottle around to the opposite side. Bring the strand on the left side around and form a loop, then insert the loop underneath the core strands.

8 | Bring the strand on the right side through the loop of the left strand, over the core strands, and then underneath the left strand.

9 | Continuing with the same strand, bring it over the core strands and through the loop of the left strand.

10 | Pull the left and right cords outward to tighten the knot.

11 | Flip the bottle around to the opposite side. Bring the strand on the right side around and form a loop, then insert the loop underneath the core strands.

12 | Bring the strand on the left side through the loop of the right strand, over the core strands, and then underneath the right strand. Bring the cord over the core strands and through the loop of the left strand.

13 | Pull the left and right cords outward to tighten the knot.

14 | Repeat steps 3 through 13, and continue tying until you've reached the bottom of the bottle. Then finish the bottle by tying a Solomon Bar (page 15) until you reach the opposite side.

15 | You will have completed the design once you have reached the opposite side with the Solomon Bar. Cut the remainder of the excess cord and melt the ends with a lighter.

Hangman's Knot

This knot can be used in applications that need a sliding loop.

1 | Form a reverse "S" with the cord.

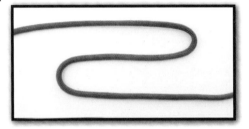

2 | Bring the upper strand underneath the lower strands and then back over the top.

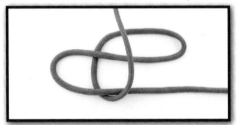

3 | Wrap the top strand around the lower strands several times.

4 | To lock the knot, insert the remaining section of the wrapped strand through the knot.

5 | Pull on the noose to tighten the knot. Cut the remainder of the excess cord and melt the ends with a lighter.

Knife Handle Wrap

The design used in this wrap was originally created by J. D. Lenzen and called "Bug Belly Bar." Make sure to tape the blade of the knife to keep from being cut. Use extreme caution when tying this design.

1 | Insert the cord through the knife handle.

2 | Bring the right strand over the handle.

3 | Bring the left strand underneath the left side of the handle, over the right strand, and then back underneath the right side of the handle.

4 | Push up and tighten the knot. Bring the right strand over the handle. Bring the left strand underneath the left side of the handle, under the right strand, and then back over the right side of the handle.

5 | Push up and tighten the knot. Bring the right strand over the handle. Bring the left strand underneath the left side of the handle, over the right strand, and then back underneath the right side of the handle. Continue tying until you've reached the bottom of the handle.

6 | Loosen the left and right sides of the cord.

7 | Insert the ends of the cord through the loops.

8 | Tighten the knots.

9 | Move up two rows from the bottom and loosen the left and right sides of the cord.

10 | Insert the ends of the cord through the loops.

11 | Tighten the knots.

12 | Continue to move up two rows and loosen the left and right sides of the cord until you've reached the top.

13 | Insert the ends of the cord through the loops. Tighten the knots. Cut the remainder of the excess cord and melt the ends with a lighter.

Monkey Chain

This simple design works well as a necklace or leash, but can be used as a bracelet.

1 | Find the middle of the cord and make a loop with the right strand crossing over the left.

2 | Make a loop with the right strand and then insert it into the loop created in step 1 to make a Slip Knot (see Chain Sinnet, page 75).

3 | Pull the knot tight by pulling on the left strand.

4 | Make a loop with the right strand and insert it through the loop on top.

5 | To start to tighten the knot, pull down on the left side of the bottom loop you just created.

6 | Now pull up on the left side of the top loop to finish tightening.

7 | Form a loop with the right cord and then insert it through the opposite loop.

8 | Tighten the knot.

9 | Form a loop with the right cord and then insert it through the opposite loop.

10 | Tighten the knot.

11 | Repeat steps 9 and 10, and continue tying until you've reached the desired length.

12 | To lock the knot, insert the entire right strand through the loop and then tighten. Cut the remainder of the excess cord and melt the ends with a lighter.

Monkey's Fist

This design can be used as a keychain decoration or even a weapon. You can use your hand instead of the tool shown below. You'll also need a marble for the core.

1 | Wrap the cord around your first four fingers three or four times.

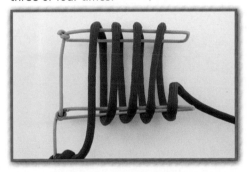

2 | Wrap the cord around the cord you just wrapped in the other direction.

3 | Insert the marble into the center and tighten the cord.

4 | Insert the cord through the center to begin wrapping the next section in the third direction.

5 | The Monkey's Fist is completed, but needs to be tightened; this is accomplished by carefully working your way back through the entire knot. This example shows the Monkey's Fist tied as a keychain. Use a Blood Knot (page 74) for the loop.

Over-Under Heaving Line Knot

As its name suggests, this was originally tied using thick rope so the line could be thrown from one boat to another.

1 | Find the middle of the cord.

2 | Form a sideways "S."

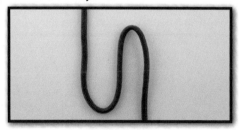

3 | Bring the left strand around and over the middle strand.

4 | Bring the same strand around the backside of the middle strand and right strand.

5 | Bring the same strand back over the right strand, over the middle strand, and over the left strand.

6 | Bring the strand around the back of the left strand and underneath the middle strand. Then wrap it around the middle strand and underneath the right strand.

7 | Bring the strand around and back over the right strand, under the middle, and then over the left strand.

8 | Repeat steps 6 and 7, and continue tying until you've reached the bottom of the loop. Pull the right strand to tighten the knot.

9 | Cut the remainder of the excess cord and then melt the ends with a lighter. Add a Hangman's Knot (page 82) to the excess length of cord for a decorative finish.

CHAPTER 5

Braids & Weaves

Four-Strand Diamond Braid

This is tied the same as the Four-Strand Spiral Braid (page 92) but is started differently. It would make a great necklace or leash.

1 | Find the middle of two strands and then interlock them.

2 | Bring the far right strand underneath the two center strands and then back over the left center strand. If tying a bracelet, loosen one of the cords to allow for a bracelet loop.

3 | Bring the far left strand underneath the two center strands and then back over the right center strand.

4 | Bring the far right strand underneath the two center strands and then back over the left center strand.

5 | Bring the far left strand underneath the two center strands and then back over the right center strand.

6 | Repeat steps 2 through 5, and continue tying until you've reached the desired length. To secure the knot, tie an Overhand Knot (page 13) with the gray cord over the two silver strands. Cut the remainder of the excess cord and melt the ends with a lighter.

Four-Strand Spiral Braid

Like the Four-Strand Diamond Braid (page 91), this makes a great necklace or leash.

1 | Find the middle of two cords and then slightly overlap them as shown.

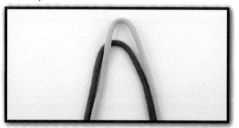

2 | Bring the far right strand underneath the two center strands and then back over the left center strand. If tying a bracelet, loosen one of the cords to allow for a bracelet loop.

3 | Bring the far left strand underneath the two center strands and then back over the right center strand.

4 | Bring the far right strand underneath the two center strands and then back over the left center strand.

5 | Bring the far left strand underneath the two center strands and then back over the right center strand.

6 | Carefully keep tension on the knots while tying. Bring the far right strand underneath the two center strands and then back over the left center strand.

7 | Bring the far left strand underneath the two center strands and then back over the right center strand.

8 | Repeat steps 6 and 7, and continue tying until you've reached the desired length. Secure the design with an Overhand Knot (page 13) on the end.

9 | Cut the remainder of the excess cord and melt the ends with a lighter.

Over-Under Weave

To tie this as a 7½-inch bracelet as shown, you'll need a shorter 24-inch strand of paracord (silver) and a longer 90-inch strand (red).

1 | Fold the short silver strand of paracord in the middle and tie a knot or Bracelet Clasp (page 11) at the end. This needs to be the size of the bracelet you intend to tie.

2 | Bring the end of the long red cord over the left silver strand, under the right silver strand, and then around and over the right strand and under the left strand.

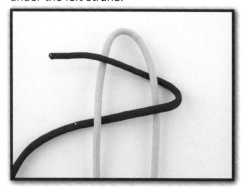

3 | Bring the red cord around and over the left silver strand and then under the right silver strand.

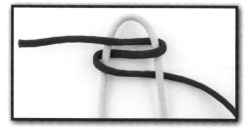

4 | To secure the top section, you will need to tuck the loose end underneath itself as shown.

5 | Bring the red cord around and over the right silver strand and then under the left silver strand.

6 | Bring the red cord around and over the left silver strand and then under the right silver strand.

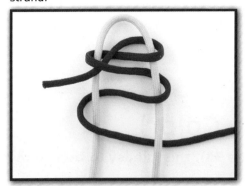

7 | Carefully tighten the red cord.

8 | Continue to bring the red cord around and over and then under the silver cord until you've reached the desired length or the knot at the end.

9 | Once you've reached the knot at the end, cut the remainder of the excess cord and melt the end with a lighter.

Over-Under Weave (Two Color)

Like the single-color Over-Under Weave (page 94), this is easy to tie and makes an attractive, comfortable bracelet.

1 | Tie a Bracelet Loop (page 10) with red and silver cords. Tighten the knot.

2 | Bring the left red strand over the silver core strand and under the red core strand.

3 | Bring the right silver strand over the red core strand, then under the silver core strand.

4 | Pull both strands tight. Bring the silver strand over the silver core strand and under the red core strand. Bring the red strand over the red core strand and under the silver core strand.

5 | Pull both strands tight. Bring the red strand over the silver core strand and under the red core strand. Bring the silver strand over the red core strand and under the silver core strand.

6 | Pull both strands tight. Bring the silver strand over the silver core strand and under the red core strand. Bring the red strand over the red core strand and under the silver core strand.

7 | Repeat steps 5 and 6, and continue tying until you've reached the desired length. Tie a Bracelet Clasp (page 11) or Overhand Knot (page 13) using the center strands. Cut the remainder of the excess cord and melt the ends with a lighter.

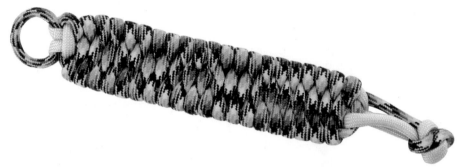

Over-Under Three-Strand Weave

This design is similar to the Over-Under Weave (page 94), but an extra strand is added to the core.

1 | Find the middle of the green cord and then bring the right side over the left.

2 | Find the middle of the white cord and bring it over the loop made with the green cord from front to back. Then bring the cord back around and over the green cord and through the loop you just made.

3 | Tighten the knot. The white cord will form two of the core strands. The third strand will be the green strand on the far left. The loop at the top of this design will be the Bracelet Loop (page 10).

4 | Start weaving by bringing the green working strand on the far right over the right core strand, under the center, and then over the left green strand.

5 | Bring the same strand around and underneath the left core strand, over the center, and then under the right core strand.

6 | Tighten the knot.

7 | Continue weaving by bringing the working strand on the right around and over the right core strand, under the center, and then over the left core strand.

8 | Bring the strand around and underneath the left core strand, over the center, and then under the right core strand.

9 | Tighten the knot. Repeat steps 7 through 8, and continue tying until you've reached the desired length.

10 | Secure the bracelet by bringing the left core strand over the center core strand and then bring the right core strand underneath the center core strand and out the loop of the left core strand, as if tying a Solomon Bar (page 15).

11 | Tighten the knot.

12 | Bring the left, center, and right cords down and use them to tie the Bracelet Clasp. In this example, the clasp is a Wall Sinnet (page 111).

13 | Tighten the knot.

14 | Add another round to the Wall Sinnet to finish the bracelet clasp. Cut the remainder of the excess cord and melt the ends with a lighter.

CHAPTER 6

Decorative Knots

Arms-Akimbo Knot

This attractive knot originally tied by John Shaw is not meant to stand alone, but to add a decorative touch to another design.

1 | Find the middle of the cord and bring the left strand over the right.

2 | Bring the right strand over and through the loop to form a Slip Knot (see Chain Sinnet, page 75).

3 | Form an "S" shape with the right, and then bring the strand underneath and through the loop of the Slip Knot.

4 | Bring the strand over to the right and through the loop formed in step 3. Carefully tighten the Slip Knot and then finish tightening the remainder of the knot.

Chinese Butterfly Knot

This knot closely resembles the Chinese Cloverleaf (page 105). The easiest way to learn to tie this design is to pin it to a corkboard and tie as shown.

1 | There are two ways this can be tied: either with two cords or one. Both begin the same way. Lay out the first cord as shown.

2 | To tie with two cords, insert the second cord (white) as shown, weaving it into the cord from step 1.

3 | Carefully tighten the cords to finish tying the Chinese Butterfly Knot.

4 | To tie with just one strand, begin the same way as the original.

5 | Bring the cord around, forming a loop, and insert it through as shown with the white cord.

6 | Carefully tighten the cord.

Chinese Cloverleaf Knot

This little knot would make an excellent zipper pull.

1 | Find the middle the of the cord.

2 | Make a loop with the left strand, then pull a second loop underneath the right strand.

3 | Wrap the left strand up and back under the right strand, then over the top and down through the second loop formed in step 2.

4 | Now bring the strand around toward the right and go over, under, over, and over through the bottom loops.

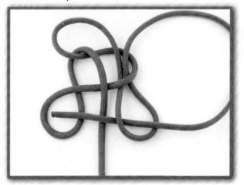

5 | Wrap the strand back toward the right and bring it underneath and then under, under, and then over and out.

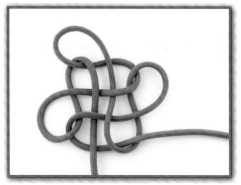

6 | Bring the strand around and up through the center by going over, under, under, over, and then under to finish. Now tighten the design to finish the knot.

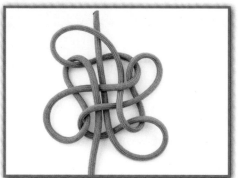

Chinese Snake Knot

This popular design can stand alone or add something special to another project. It would make a great small bracelet or necklace, or even a zipper pull or keychain.

1 | With the two strands side by side, bring the right blue strand underneath and then over the gray strand and up, forming a loop.

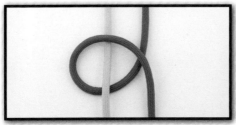

2 | Now bring the gray strand over and then underneath the blue strand and then out and down, forming a loop.

3 | Loosely tighten the knots.

4 | Bring the blue strand back around the gray strand and through the gray loop and down, and tighten.

5 | Flip the knot over.

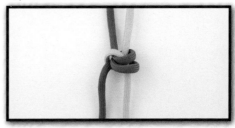

6 | Bring the gray strand (now on the right) back around the blue strand and down through the loop, and tighten.

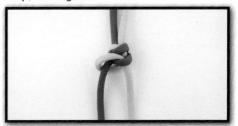

7 | Flip the knot over.

8 | Bring the blue strand on the right back around the gray strand and through the loop and tighten. Continue flipping over and tightening until you have reached the desired length. To finish the design as shown in this example, make a loop with the remaining cord and tie a Blood Knot (page 74). Cut the remainder of the excess cord and melt the ends with a lighter.

Cross Knot

Use this knot as a loop to start another design, or continue tying Cross Knots to make a bracelet.

1 | Find the middle of the cord, then bring the left strand over and under the right strand.

2 | Bring the right strand up and under the two parts of the left strand, and then down and over both.

3 | Bring the left strand over, over, and then under and out. Tighten the knot to finish.

Matthew Walker Knot

This is a decorative knot that can be used in different ways. It can add a decorative touch to the middle of two strands, and it can also be used as a Bracelet Clasp.

1 | Place the two strands side by side and fold them down at the point that you intend to tie the knot.

2 | Bring the left strand over the center strands and under the right strand.

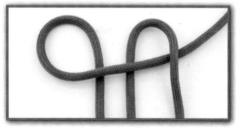

3 | Bring the right strand underneath the center strands and out the loop of the left strand.

4 | Continuing with the right strand, bring it over the center strands and under and out the loop.

5 | With the left strand (now on the right side), bring it around and underneath the center strands and out the loop. Carefully twist and pull on both ends to finish off the knot.